HOW TO CHIP LIKE A PRO

IN 4 SIMPLE STEPS

by Frank Muir

Published by JHJ22 Publishing

Copyright © Frank Muir 2015

ISBN(13) 978-1-5151447-9-3

ISBN (10) 1-5151447-9-8

TABLE OF CONTENTS

CHAPTER 1

INTRODUCTION

If you're reading this self-help booklet it's because you're struggling to get up and down in two from around the greens. You're leaving so many strokes out there on the golf course that it hurts when you drown your sorrows at the 19th. Or maybe you're looking for some way to improve on your already tight short game, pick up some tip that will perk up your attitude around the greens, and shave a stroke or three off your scores. Whatever your reason, this self-help booklet will introduce you to four simple steps that will have your short game so sharp you could cut your fingers pulling your wedge from the bag.

And you won't have to spend another cent. No expensive sessions with your local golf pro, or even worse, sports psychologist. For way less than a ticket to the movies, you have purchased this self-help booklet that will show you how to chip around the greens like a pro. In other words, this is money well spent.

It doesn't matter if you're fluffing, skinning, or skying your chips from around the greens, my 4-step process will have you strutting with confidence when your ball rolls off the putting surface to rest by the edge of the green, because you believe you will have a better chance of chipping in than holing out a long putt. My 4-step process will transform your chipping beyond all recognition. You will soon chip with confidence, no longer simply chipping the ball in the general direction of the hole, but actually aiming to hole it, with the confidence to believe that you really can! To accomplish this, I am going to take you to the very heart of your problem – *you* – and sort you out.

CHAPTER 2

WHO AM I?

First of all let me tell you who I am not. I am not a professional golfer, or internet whiz-kid intent on screwing you out of your money. I am just a regular guy – a lot older than I'd like to be! – who once played golf to a fairly decent level, but who suffered from all kinds of golfing ailments over the years. With persistence and time, I overcame these ailments – some allegedly *incurable* – mostly by trial and error, and I now want to share these secrets to help other 'broken' golfers.

In the end, over the years, I came to understand that the longest and most difficult shot in golf is the six inches between the ears. For me, Tiger nailed the true definition of golf when he said – ***golf is a game of mental toughness***. Boy, did he get that right. At the time of writing this booklet, Tiger has just dropped out of the world's top 100 for the first time in his career. I believe little has changed in Tiger's physical game, but his mental strength and self-belief – once so powerful that not only did he believe he was invincible as a golfer, he had the rest of the professionals believing it too – has taken a hit. That's how important these six inches are.

If you purchased my first self-help booklet – *How to cure your putting yips in 4 simple steps* – you will have read about my own personal struggles to overcome my golf game. In that booklet I said – *the loss of confidence on the greens will almost certainly over time spread into every aspect of the golfer's game*. And sure enough, when my putting began to deteriorate, I found that my short game – the shots a golfer makes that do not require a full swing, but primarily rely on touch – fell away, too. I don't like the phrase *chipping yips*, but I suppose that's what I had. My putting yips had overcome my mind so strongly that any other short shot around the green would have me gritting my teeth and sweating like a wrestler stepping into an alligator pit. I was a nervous wreck when it came to anything other than a full shot, and around the greens I was a mess. My chips were no longer aimed at getting the ball close to the hole, but nothing more than a nervous attempt just to hit the ball without fluffing or skinning it, and get it onto the green somewhere – *anywhere* – in the general direction of the hole.

But throughout all these yipping woes, I continued to be a solid striker of the ball. I could drive the ball as far as the next golfer, or hit a long iron like a pro. My long game kept me going for a while, and I could shoot the odd low round by hitting plenty of greens and making a few putts. But as soon as I missed a green, I knew with certainty that I was about to drop a shot against par.

I had a history of playing golf then giving it up for some years before coming back to it again. And every time I returned to the game, the old woes were still present. Although I'd cured my putting yips and was considered to be a damn good putter

– one low handicapper once told me if he ever had to stake his life on someone holing a four-footer, he would choose me to take that putt! – I was still woeful around the greens. But it wasn't until much later in life – maybe because I had mellowed some, and golf could no longer drive me wild the way it used to! – that I came upon a cure for my chipping.

In this booklet, I will explain to you how I tackled these *six inches between the ears*, and changed my attitude to chip shots around the green, so that I no longer feared them, but relished making them. My 4-step process will show you how you, too, can overcome your fears, and make your short game as sharp as any pro's. You will be amazed by how improved your chipping will become. Believe me, this self-help manual will change your chipping ability beyond all recognition. I know it will. If it worked for me, then it can work for you.

At the end of this booklet you will find my website address, and you can learn a bit more about me and what I now do for a living. Feel free to contact me if you want, hopefully to tell me you are no longer despondent when you miss the green, and you really are now chipping like a pro.

CHAPTER 3

WHAT IS A CHIP SHOT?

For the purposes of this booklet, it is important for the golfer to understand what we mean when we use the term 'chip shot.' Webster's new Twentieth Century Dictionary defines a 'chip shot' as – *in golf, a short, lofting stroke, used when the ball is near the green.* The important point to note here is that the ball is *near the green.* Throughout this manual, wherever I use the term *around the green*, I am referring to shots close to the putting surface, the result of some approach shot, for example, that has only just missed the green, or rolled off the putting surface, to finish up on the apron, or short grass close to it – no more than ten feet or so from the edge of the green. The chip shot is distinctly different from a *pitch*, where the golfer might use a wedge to *pitch* the ball onto the green from, say, some fifty yards or so distant.

So, what's the problem with chipping the ball onto the green? After all, you're probably close enough to the hole to take two putts – if your ball had been on the putting surface instead of having missed it! It should be a simple matter to chip the ball close to the hole, then nail the putt – in other words, to get up and down in two. But most amateur golfers can't manage that. Somehow, when they have a lofted club in their hand so close to the putting surface, the simple chip shot takes on a whole new complexion. But many of these shots are no longer than a longish putt, and would be holed in two if the golfer used his putter. And that's what the golfer mostly does – reaches for his putter, instead of taking the correct club. The end result? Up and down in three.

And here's the reason why.

The root cause of the golfer struggling with these types of chip shots is that he has to rely on touch. He can't just stand up and take a full swing at it, but like putting, has to rely on fine motor control skills. The problem with that is these skills are governed by what's going on between the ears. Through your own personal experience of having struggled with these shots time and time before – fluffed, or skinned them – over the years you have 'taught' yourself to fear them. Your mind has now become conditioned to respond in a negative way when you prepare to commit to a chip shot. Faced with a simple chip shot, the golfer's most common course of action is to compound the problem, by choosing the wrong club for the shot.

Think about that for a moment. You've been there before, faced with a shot that is no more than four feet off the putting surface, tantalisingly close to the green. But instead of choosing a lofted club, you go for what you think is the percentage shot and pull your putter from the bag. You line up the 'putt' and give it a solid hit. But the length and texture of the grass around the greens is typically nothing like the putting surface, and more often than not you over- or under-compensate in the weight, resulting in your ball rolling way past the hole, or coming up far too short. You almost never get the weight of that shot spot on, and instead of having a tap-in putt, you're now faced with an eight- to ten-footer to save par.

This self-help booklet will help you overcome your learned fear of this simple chip shot, by showing you how to choose the correct club and take the correct stance, make the correct action for the shot, as well as conditioning your mind to *change your chipping attitude*, enabling you to remain calm and focused when you prepare to chip.

So, read on.

CHAPTER 4

STEP 1

CHOOSE THE CORRECT CLUB

When faced with a chip shot from the edge of the green, most golfers will reach for their putter and use it as a *Texas wedge* by putting onto the green. There are a couple of problems with this method. Firstly, the difference in speed between the green and the longer fairway grass makes estimating the weight of the putt more guesswork and luck, than putting skill. Secondly, the first few feet of that putt is made over ground that is typically not as smooth as the green. This results in inconsistent off-green putts with diminished accuracy, leaving the golfer more often than not farther from the hole than desired, and facing a missable putt for par.

The key to improving accuracy and consistency from around the greens, is not to use the putter, but to select the correct club for the shot. And here's how to do that.

We've all seen the pros take a full swing by the edge of the green – the ball pops up almost vertically, to land close to the hole. These chip shots are spectacular to watch, jaw-droppingly stunning when pulled off, but so difficult to perform that I would urge you not to even consider them. No, the way to improve your chipping is to hit the ball with the minimum lofted club that will get it onto the green in the shortest possible distance. Sound simple? Well it is, and I want you to read that sentence over and over, again and again, until you completely understand what it means – *the way to improve your chipping is to hit the ball with **the minimum lofted club** that will get it onto the green **in the shortest possible distance**.*

I can hear you now, moaning that using a lofted club from such short distances off the green will only make it much more difficult to get up and down in two, and any numb-nut dumb-ass would putt the damn thing instead. But you're wrong. Trust me on that. And here's why.

Many amateur golfers, when they chip around the greens, break their wrists as they perform that shot. And just like in putting, breaking the wrists introduces a whole series of other problems, particularly in line and weight. But in a chip shot, breaking the wrists also increases the chances of fluffing or skinning the ball. The main reason they break their wrists, is because they have selected the wrong club – a club with too much loft – and they hit the ball harder than they should, trying to lob it into the air and land it somewhere closer to the pin than necessary. So how do you select the correct club for the shot?

I'll show you how.

Remember the first rule of the chip shot? – *hit the ball with **the minimum lofted club** that will get it onto the green **in the shortest possible distance**.* So, which club do you use from the fourteen clubs in your bag? To simplify club selection, for chip shots I use the 4-6-8-10 selection, meaning I will use only one of four lofted clubs – 4-iron for chips where the ball is closest to the green, and my 10-iron, or wedge, for chips farthest from the green. Of course, the greens invariably have slopes and humps and hollows all around them, but for the purposes of this booklet, we will work on the premise that the putting surface, and the ground surrounding it, is flat and level.

So, which of these four clubs would you select? Here are some useful guidelines to assist in your selection.

- Where the ball is closest to the green, use a 4-iron to chip onto the putting surface, and let the ball roll all the way to the hole.
- Use a 6-iron where the ratio of the flight of the ball to the roll of the ball is 1:3 – which means, if the ball is 24 feet from the hole, a

6-iron chip shot will fly the ball 6 feet, and roll it 18 feet.

- Use an 8-iron where that ratio is 1:2 – meaning, an 8-iron will fly the ball 8 feet, and roll it 16 feet.
- Use a 10-iron, or wedge, where that ratio is 1:1 – meaning, a wedge will fly the ball 12 feet, and roll it 12 feet.

It is important to understand that these distances are only a guide, and that you should spend time around the practice green chipping each of these clubs to get a feel for the different flights and lengths of run of each. A good drill to begin with, is to take 12 balls and lay them in a row no more than a foot or so from the edge of the practice green, fairly close to each other, so that each chip shot is roughly the same. Now chip 3 balls with each of your four different clubs. Watch how the balls roll more with the lesser lofted clubs, and try to develop some sense of length of flight versus roll for each of your four chipping clubs. Pay close attention to where you have to land the ball for it to run the correct distance to the hole.

However, the cure to almost all golf problems relies on the fundamentals of the game. So it doesn't matter how well you understand the flight to roll ratio – if you don't have the correct set-up for the chip shot, you will never achieve the consistency and accuracy you need to start shaving strokes off your scores.

So, read on.

CHAPTER 5

STEP 2

ADOPT THE CORRECT ACTION

So, now you have the correct club in your hand, and after a bit of practice you have a good feel for how far the ball will fly with each club, and how far it will roll. But you'll probably have found during that first practice drill that it was all a bit hit-and-miss, that some balls rolled too far, while others came up too short, or you fluffed one or two, maybe even skinned a couple. In fact, the drill session felt so wrong that you just wanted to jack in the whole stupid idea right there, and get back to using your putter.

Well don't reach for the putter. You're about to fix all of that.

So, how do you improve accuracy and consistency in these shots? The answer to that is to adopt the correct action, a chipping style that doesn't require you to break your wrists while taking the shot. The way to do that is to effectively *putt* the ball with a lofted iron. That's right. You read that correctly, and you should read it again – you will effectively **putt the ball with a lofted iron**.

I can just about hear your groans of complaint – how can you putt a ball using a lofted club? The answer is simple. **Don't break your wrists**. Understand that chip shots are soft shots made around the green, shots that require fine motor control skills, and do not require a lot of effort. If you go back to the basic premise and the first rule of the chip shot, which is to – *hit the ball with **the minimum lofted club** that will get it onto the green in the shortest possible distance*, you will see that a chip shot takes no more effort than if you were making a putt. So why not effectively putt the ball with a lofted club? If you try this, you will see that the resulting swing is almost identical to that of a putt, **but**... – isn't there always a but? – with a few basic changes in the way you address the ball, and take your stance. And here's how to do it.

I deliberately used the phrase *effectively putt the ball*, because you won't be putting the ball, of course, but chipping it with an action similar to, but slightly different from, that of a putt. So, to begin with, stand with your feet no more than shoulder-width apart, with an imaginary ball in the middle of your stance. Adjust your body so that your stance is slightly open, meaning that your feet are aiming left of the pin – the opposite is true if you play golf left-handed, of course!! Now take your selected club and hold it with a light but firm grip – this will limit the build-up in tension of the hands and arms – and choke down on the grip just a tad, meaning, shift your grip down the shaft, so that the club feels as if it is a bit shorter. Now, instead of having your weight evenly spread on both feet as you would during a putt, you need to adjust your body – again just a tad – so that you have more weight on your left leg than on your right – maybe 60% on your left, and 40% on your right. Also, position your hands slightly ahead of the ball, so that the club shaft is closer to your left thigh than your right. This is the fundamental stance for taking any chip shot.

Now what I want you to do, is to simply practice a pendulum swing back and through, back and through – the backswing more or less the same length as the follow-through – letting your hands and arms and mind become accustomed to the downward hitting of the imaginary ball. And make sure you eliminate head movement from your chipping stroke. Your head must remain still at all times, and the stroke should be little more than a rocking of your shoulders – which will open up to face the hole on completion of the chip shot, particularly on longer chips – and importantly, with *no breaking of your wrists*.

Let me emphasize that – ***Do not break your wrists during a chip shot***. Switch on the TV and tune into the Golf Channel, if you don't believe me. Watch

21

the pros make a greenside chip. Their wrists remain solid throughout the shot. So, read that phrase over and over, again and again, until you completely understand what it means. ***Do not break your wrists*** *during a chip shot*. Your stroke will be a pendulum, a rocking of your shoulders with your head still, your weight favoring your left side, your hands closer to your left thigh, and no breaking of the wrists. At the end of the chip shot, your shoulders will naturally open – because your feet are aiming left of the pin – so that you're partially facing the hole. Spend a few minutes working on that swing. Let your mind and your arms and hands become accustomed to the action, the slight downward motion of the club as it clips the ground where the ball should be, and the follow-through – typically no longer than the backswing – with your body turning just a tad to face the hole as you complete the shot.

Once you feel you've got a handle on that chipping action, read on.

CHAPTER 6

THE CORRECT ATTITUDE

Why is attitude important? Well, here's why.

Think about it. You've been there before. You've got a short iron in your hand, and you're looking to pitch the ball onto the green from, say, eighty yards or so. The way ahead is clear to an open green, and not a bunker in sight. You've got birdie ringing up all over your brain. All you have to do is lay this one close to the hole, then nail the putt. Simple, isn't it? Then you take the shot and watch in despair as your ball flies wide and misses the green to finish pin-high, six feet off the putting surface. Without fail, your very next thought is a negative one – *you're going to bogey the hole, instead of birdieing it*. Well, maybe for most amateurs it would be, although some would believe they could chip and putt for their par, get up and down in two. But if I were a betting man, I would bet the farm that you would never once think of still making that birdie. Am I right? You know I am. Well, whenever I miss a green, my first thought is – right, let's chip this in.

That's the attitude I want you to have. And that's the attitude this booklet will show you how to achieve. I'm going to start by telling you a story that will open your eyes and mind to a different perception, one you should adopt whenever you are faced with a greenside chip shot.

Years ago, when I used to play a lot of competitive golf, I was playing in the monthly medal with a youngster who could hit the ball a mile. We came to a long par 4 and the kid hammered this glorious drive down the middle of the fairway, leaving no more than a firm 9-iron to the heart of the green. It was a terrific shot, and I could tell from the way he strode down that fairway that the only thing on his mind was to make a birdie three – at a hole that historically yielded the fewest birdies on the course. Well, he took aim with his 9-iron and launched this high-flying shot that drifted just a tad on the breeze, took an awkward bounce when it landed on the green, and rolled off the putting surface, to finish up about six feet off the green. I didn't say anything. I just watched him pick up his bag and walk towards the green, no longer striding down the fairway with nothing but birdie in his sights, but with his head down, his body language telling me that he was preparing to drop a stroke to par. So, me being me, I had to intervene.

I caught up with him and asked him what was so bad about that shot. He looked at me like I was crazy, and reminded me that he'd missed the green with a stupid little 9-iron. So I decided to change his perception of the shot – change his attitude about his upcoming chip, if you like – and asked him how he would feel if he'd hit his second shot not with a 9-iron, but with a utility club from a tight lie 260 yards down the fairway and the ball had ended up lying where it did now, six feet off the green. You'd want to chip it in for a birdie, I said, and watched my message filter through his mind, knowing he was taking it in.

I would be lying if I told you he chipped in, but in the space of a few seconds, his whole attitude to the shot changed. As it was, he chipped up stone dead and had a tap-in for a par. Not quite the birdie he'd imagined as he'd stood with his 9-iron in his hand. But you get the gist of what I'm saying, I'm sure.

That is why attitude is important, and why the longest and most difficult shot is the six inches between the ears. That is what is so contrary about the game of golf. Two people can be faced with the same identical chip shot – one carrying a load of negativity about how the ball ended up there, and the other just bursting with positivity. They're both facing the exact same shot, but one is looking to get up and down in two, maybe even hole it, while the other has already marked his card with a bogy. It is important to understand that it doesn't matter a damn how the ball got there. What matters is what you're going to do with it next. And with a positive attitude, you're not thinking bogey, maybe not even par. You're thinking you're going to chip it in and make a birdie after all. But how can you improve your chipping to the point where you expect to hole shots from off the green?

Here's how.

The way to creating a positive attitude to your chipping, is to gain confidence in your ability. And the way to do that is to remove all negative thinking from the shot and allow your reflexes and muscle memory to take over on automatic and get the job done. I want you to read that sentence again and again, and one more time for luck. In fact, I want you to read that sentence as many times as necessary until you understand what it means, and what you are trying to do, which is – *to remove all negative thinking from the shot and* **allow your reflexes and muscle memory to take over on automatic** *and get the job done.*

So how do you do that?

Solid fundamentals are the key to improving your chipping. You now have the correct club, the correct stance, and the correct action. What I am now going to show you is how to build up so much confidence in your chipping ability, that you'll be looking forward to missing the greens, so you can show off to your golfing buddies, and chip it in.

And you do that by developing muscle memory.

CHAPTER 7

STEP 3

DEVELOP YOUR CHIPPING MUSCLE MEMORY

How many chip shots do you think you'd have to take before your mind and body begins to develop a sense of muscle memory, so that you could make a perfect chip every time without thinking about it? I really don't know, but for argument's sake let's say that you had to take one thousand chips before you developed reasonable muscle memory.

One thousand? That sounds like one hell of a lot of chips, doesn't it?

Well, the problem with chipping during a round of golf, is that most of us never hit enough chips to develop a feel for the shot. You may miss twelve or more of the eighteen greens, and you either putt it onto the green, hack it from the rough, or play it out of a bunker. In other words, for every eighteen holes of golf you play, you might have no more than ten chips, absolute max – and probably a lot less – around the greens. In that case it would take you one hundred rounds to make one thousand chips. And with two rounds a week, it would take you a year to hit that many chip shots. But I'm assuming you want to be able to chip like a pro in a few weeks.

So, read on.

In my first self-help booklet – *How to cure your putting yips in 4 simple steps* – I stressed the importance of developing muscle memory, so that your mind and body take the shot without you even thinking about it. In that booklet I stated that *your goal is to remove all negative thinking from the putt and* **allow your reflexes and muscle memory to take over on automatic** *and get the job done*. You have to do exactly the same with your chips shots, if you want to chip like a pro.

And here's how to do that.

I want you to find a spot in your home where you can place a ball on the carpet and chip it against something soft. What I do is turn one of our sofas around so that I can chip into the back of it. That way, the ball does not rebound too hard. Once you've worked something out in your own home, I want you to place a ball on the carpet no more than three feet from whatever you've set up – mattress, pillows, cushions, back of sofa, or whatever. Now take your highest lofted club – your wedge – and chip the ball into this 'soft wall' so that it bounces back. This way, you don't have to disrupt your practice session while you run after the ball to hit it again. This simple method is key to developing muscle memory for your chip shots – the repetitive striking of the ball, using the same stroke again and again and again, with the ball returning each time, to be nudged onto the same spot, then chipped once more, and all done *without breaking your wrists*.

NOTE: I suggest using a wedge to begin with for this drill, as the ball will fly into the 'soft wall' and bounce back. You'll find that once you become competent with this shot, all other chip shots with lesser lofted clubs will be so much easier.

Now, what if I said that you could hit one thousand chips in less than two hours? – under one hour and thirty minutes, in my case. Would that convince you that developing muscle memory to chip like a pro is well within your reach?

I bet you it does. And here's how to do that.

Go back to placing a ball no more than three feet from the 'soft wall,' and take your stance. Now chip that ball into the 'soft wall,' letting it bounce back to you each time, then nudging it back onto its spot for you to chip again. It's important to understand that you are not going for accuracy here, nor are you spending too much time over each chip. It doesn't matter if you start by thinning a few chips, or duffing a few, or that it all feels odd. It matters only that you continue to chip that ball again and again, knowing that each chip is sending one more message to your brain, logging it into your subconscious where it will be stored for later use. It's also important to understand that doing this drill in this quick and repetitive manner will not allow your mind to 'lock' onto the chip, but will rid it of any subconscious need to freeze over the shot.

I don't expect you to stand up against that 'soft wall' for a couple of hours. Doing that would have you quitting right there. No, I want you to take fifty chips only, and I want you to time yourself. It takes me around four minutes to take 50 chip shots, bouncing them off the back of the sofa like that, and I want you to aim for about that length of time, too. Now, once you've timed yourself, multiply that time by 20, and that will tell you how long it will take you to make one thousand chips. In other words, if you do that 50-chip routine twenty times, you will have made one thousand chips. But more importantly, you will have sent one thousand messages to your brain telling it how to perform a chip shot, preparing it to *allow your reflexes and muscle memory to take over on automatic*.

Once you've done your first fifty chips, I want you to take a break. Have a juice. Go out for a walk. Take a breath of fresh air. Do twenty press-ups. Do something, anything, to break the monotony of the routine. Continue if you like, carry on for another fifty or more, but I've found the 50-chip routine lets me fit it in anytime I like during my working day. I don't care how busy you claim to be. If you can't find time in a 24-hour day to take a 4-minute break, then you can't find time to play golf at all – period – so the exercise is meaningless anyway.

So, getting back to that first 50 chips, it's important not to worry that it all feels different and clumsy, chipping a wedge off the carpet, or that you're thinning a few chips and duffing others, or that it's not going to work. Do not worry. It will work. Trust me on that. I have no doubts at all, and neither will you after you've performed a number of 50-chip sessions.

In my other self-help booklet – *How to cure your putting yips in 4 simple steps* – I stated that it took me somewhere in the region of 500 putts before I had that first hint of a sense that I might finally be overcoming my putting yips. In the case of my chipping, my negative thoughts and bad technique had become so deeply ingrained into my being that it took me somewhere in excess of 1,500 chips – just bouncing that ball off the back of the sofa, time and time again, on and on and on – until I began to have a sense that I could be cured. 1,500 chip shots? That's one hell of a lot of chipping. But in truth, it took me little more than 2 hours in total to accomplish that. If I told you that you could chip like a pro in around 2 hours, would you jump at it? You bet you would. You would jump straight in with both feet.

What I like most about this 50-chip drill is that it takes no time at all to complete – around four minutes in my case – and that each 50-chip session can be done anytime you like, and without having to leave home. First thing in the morning as soon as you get out of bed, then another 50 chips after you have a shower. Do a quick 50-chip session before breakfast, and another after, and you've completed 200 chip shots before you've even left home for the office. Do that every day, and you've done 1,500 chips in just over a week. See how quickly you can rack up the number of chips? But importantly, every single chip shot you make into that 'soft wall' is sending one more signal to your brain, setting it up to *allow your reflexes and muscle memory to take over on automatic*.

This 50-chip practice drill really does work.

But you're not done yet.

CHAPTER 8

STEP 4

DEVELOP YOUR CHIPPING CONFIDENCE

So, you're now able to face that 'soft wall' and make 50 chips into it time and time again with all the confidence in the world. Now comes the true test, taking what you've practiced at home – the correct stance, the correct action, the correct attitude, the developed muscle memory – and trying it for real on the golf course.

But I know as you walk toward that first tee, you will have a real sense of worry, maybe even a fear, that it won't work, that it's all very well doing it at home, but when it comes to the golf course, that's different. Well, understand that it will work. Trust yourself. Believe in your ability. Your mind and body are working together now through self-taught muscle memory. But before you hit that first drive, eager to get into the round and start chipping your golf balls stiff, I want you to spend some time on the practice green. I am about to introduce you to one more practice drill that will improve your chipping ability beyond all recognition.

Here's how to do it.

What you have to do if you want to chip like a pro, is to make your mind believe you can hole chips from anywhere around the green. And to do that, you have to practice holing out chips. I can't impress enough upon you how important this is – *you must practice **holing out chips***. So before you rush onto that first tee, go to the practice green, and select a hole on a relatively flat part of the green, and one that is quite close to the edge of the green – you're not going for difficulty here, just trying to train your mind into believing that you can hole chips. Now place a half a dozen balls at the edge of the green, no more than six inches from it, and take your 4-iron and start chipping them to the hole. Take your time over each chip, making sure you have a slightly open stance, weight forward just a touch, hands ahead of the ball a tad, just as you've done a thousand times at home, and *effectively putt* each ball into the hole. It doesn't matter if the hole is only four feet from the edge of the green – in fact, for this exercise, the shorter the chip, the better – what you are trying to accomplish is to establish firmly in the depths of your subconscious that you can chip balls from off the green into the hole. Believe me when I say – once you begin to hole a few of these short chips, you will want to try longer chip shots to prove to yourself that you really can do it. But most importantly, by consistently holing out from just off the green, you are cementing in your brain your ability to chip in from any distance.

The strength of this drill is that it consolidates all you have learned in developing your chipping muscle memory, while giving you a taste of what it feels like when you hole a chip shot. Importantly, it builds up confidence, changes your belief, and generates a positive attitude. You will no longer fear missing the green. You will no longer worry about dropping a shot to par. You will become so confident in your chipping ability that you will truly believe you can chip the ball into the hole from anywhere close to the green. In fact, I've seen me striding up to the green after I've had a weak approach shot, hoping that my ball is resting on the apron because I know I have a better chance of chipping it in than holing a long putt!

And this practice drill before each round takes no time at all. You don't need to arrive for your scheduled round an hour or so early. All it takes is a few minutes, ten tops, to give your hands and arms and mind the exhilarating feeling of chipping in, and importantly, stimulating that muscle memory.

Now go out there and play golf without any fear of dropping shots around the greens. What have you to be afraid of? It doesn't matter how the ball got there. It matters only that you now know how to chip it in. So look forward to laying these chips stone dead, leaving nothing but a tap-in, and from time to time just chipping the ball straight into the hole. Take your stance, and trust your action.

Don't even think about it. You've assigned it to muscle memory.

But remember that golf is a game. Play it for exercise and fun. You won't hole every chip, and you won't leave them all stone dead either. But with your new chipping action and confidence, you're giving yourself every chance to do so. So go out there and enjoy your golf. If you miss the green, relish the challenge of chipping in. Believe in your chipping ability, and prove to yourself – and your golfing buddies – that you can chip as well as the best of them.

In fact, show them how you can now chip like a pro.

CHAPTER 9

ABOUT THE AUTHOR

Although Frank used to be a keen golfer, he is now more of an armchair sportsman than a participant, yet he continues to proclaim his natural ability to birdie the 19th hole with astonishing regularity.

Born far too many years ago in Scotland, Frank graduated from Strathclyde University, Glasgow, with a degree he hated. He assures everyone who cares to listen, that he never really wanted to be a civil engineer, but with youthful apathy soon found himself working in Glasgow's Department of Architecture and Related Services designing sewerage schemes, and wondering how in the hell he got there, and what did he really want to do with his life. Working overseas sounded like a good idea, so off he went to the Middle East – Saudi Arabia, Qatar, Bahrain – then the USA, where he worked and lived for over 20 years, regrettably as a civil engineer.

But living and working overseas helped Frank appreciate the raw beauty of his home country, and his love of reading fiction helped him understand that his true calling was to be a novelist. Now a dual US/UK citizen, Frank makes his home in the outskirts of Glasgow, where he writes his best-selling crime series set in – where else? – St. Andrews, the home of golf. Frank can often be seen carrying out some serious research in the old grey town's many pubs, all under the guise of practicing that 19th hole. Despite that, Frank assures his wife that he is working hard on his next crime novel.

Visit Frank's website at www.frankmuir.com for details of his crime novels. Frank writes under the author name of T.F. Muir in the UK, and T. Frank Muir in the USA, and maintains that multiple author names are almost as confusing as civil engineering.

CHAPTER 10
OTHER BOOKS WRITTEN BY FRANK

Fiction:

Frank's DCI Andy Gilchrist crime series set in St. Andrews, Scotland.

Author name – T.F. Muir

*Eye for an Eye * §*

*Hand for a Hand * §*

*Tooth for a Tooth **

*Life for a Life **

The Meating Room

* Also published in the USA under the author name T. Frank Muir

§ Also published in the UK under the author name Frank Muir

Self-help:

Author name – Frank Muir

How to Cure your Putting Yips – in 4 Simple Steps

www.frankmuir.com

21441124R00029

Printed in Poland
by Amazon Fulfillment
Poland Sp. z o.o., Wrocław